Franklin Feldman

Selected Graphic Work

1958-2004

Franklin Feldman

SELECTED GRAPHIC WORK

1958-2004

WITH ESSAYS BY

Janis Conner

Kathy Caraccio

Indian Mountain Press

Library of Congress Cataloging-in-Publication Data

Feldman, Franklin.
Selected graphic work of Franklin Feldman, 1958-2004 / with essays by Janis Conner and Kathy Caraccio.
p. cm.
ISBN 0-9661239-1-3
1. Feldman, Franklin—Catalogs. I. Conner, Janis C. II. Caraccio, Kathleen. III. Title.
NE539.F444A4 2004
769.92—dc22 2004065785

Designed by Joan O'Connor.

for Naomi

my indispensable
critic and most
ardent supporter

Contents

Our lives, we say, are full of "issues," a knowing term that describes anything from dark neuroses to charming eccentricities. It is a word used loosely to suggest the unfinished business of the psyche, with its unravelings and longings, its memories, veiled or examined. From the primary elements of life–sex, family, work, and mortality–artists create something palpable and lasting, and leave us to decipher their messages.

Franklin Feldman takes issue with "issues," and the suggestion that he too has them evokes one of his serial responses: "What issues? What do you mean by issues? What kind of issues?" Frank often tweaks one's questions, digs around them to unearth the reason for the query. His stubborn but good-humored response to the subject is, "I don't have issues. I just make art." But it is through his art, of course, that he continually examines and reviews his life. *Anna* (p.108) is an aquatint I find especially affecting, and when I inquired of him, "Why 'Anna?,'" I received a shrug. "No particular reason." Going on to say that Anna was my favorite name, Frank added matter-of-factly, "It was my mother's name." I decided to probe no further, not to ask if this was indeed an image of his mother or a memento of some kind. But his response was intriguing, if not baffling, and I gave myself permission to speculate.

While object-based images are often descriptively titled, artists often avoid evocative language in order to reinforce abstraction. That Frank chooses to fasten expressive titles to nearly all his pictures, indicates his pleasure in naming his work, his desire to interpret it for himself. Whatever the case, he enjoys naming his handiwork. The aquatint called *Press Me Fondly* (p.23) is a potent, representational emblem of the life force the artist finds in art, while its deliciously punning title suggests the intimacy and tenderness expressed in the act of creation.

Like so many artists, Frank has made art since he was a youngster, attending New York City's High School of Music and Art, later continuing his studies at the Art Students League from 1955 to 1965. As a mature artist, he has continued to attend art classes at the Pratt Graphic Center, as well as The New School (Parsons Division), where his principal instructors have been John Ross and Herman Zaage. Frank maintained his art studies while an undergraduate at New York University and then at Columbia Law School, where his academic excellence was recognized with appointment to editor-in-chief of the *Columbia Law Review*. Soon after earning his law degree, Frank began an accomplished career with the distinguished firm of Stroock & Stroock & Lavan, where he specialized in corporate and commodities law. In the early 1960s he became interested in the emerging subject of art law, in which he developed an expertise, and he soon became a principal practitioner in the field. He established at Columbia Law School with the late Kirk Varnedoe, a graduate seminar on art law that he continued to teach for twenty-three years. He co-authored with Stephen Weil, the two-volume treatise, *Art Law*. Published by Little, Brown, & Co., it was an important contribution to a subject that has since gained much public, as well as legal attention. The book was given the Scribes Award for the best law book of 1986 and continues in use as a reference and textbook.

Throughout his law career, art provided Frank ongoing creative stimulation. When he retired from the law in 1989, art became his daily practice, discipline, and pleasure. This selection of images represents forty-seven years of his prolific printmaking, the medium he finds most satisfying through its variety of production and effects, and the opportunities it affords for experimentation and serendipity. His favored method is to draw spontaneously, to allow intuition to guide his hand across the plate or paper, resulting in a fluid, often rhythmic style that suggests the influence of the brilliant technician and innovator, Stanley William Hayter. During the war, the British-born artist temporarily moved his studio, Atélier 17, to New York, where he worked and taught from 1941 to 1950, influencing a generation of American artists. Hayter's groundbreaking technical developments as well as his style, a Surrealism-based abstraction, had a seminal influence on printmaking. Frank's method frequently employs the intuitive, primal gesture as the originating source for the image, which he then consciously elaborates upon. Like a musician or dancer whose acquired technique provides a solid foundation just beneath the surface of a moving, interpretive performance, a visual artist's distinctive line is his means to convey emotion.

An early etching and aquatint called *Two Faces* (p.87) begins with a ground of mottled color and large, empty areas, most prominent of which are three moon-like circles. Two are given faces, the lower one loosely and quickly rendered, its three-quarter profile averted and self-absorbed. The upper face, its features executed with more detail, looks directly at us with one knowing eye, while ignoring us with the other. Frank's earliest self-portrait (p.2) also has an averted gaze, the left side obscured by shadow suggesting an unfinished aspect that is underscored by its abbreviated title, *Self-P, as Young M*.

In 1970, Frank began a series of works based on family photographs.

A recurring and important theme, familial imagery provides a vehicle for the artist's exploration of printmaking techniques as well as for personal history. Interpretations of pre-existing pictures, they may express deep feeling, but they never veer into sentimentality. Titles often identify the subjects' relationships to each other or to the artist, thereby generating an aura of intimacy. Settings and poses may be manipulated to add a layer of ambiguity, for example: what inspired *Grandpa in a Tree?* (p.8) His demeanor makes the situation seem commonplace, and with Grandma leaning against the tree's low, strong branches, their roles as patriarch and matriarch of the family hierarchy are deftly symbolized. This etching and aquatint is one of my favorite prints, and Frank's grandpa has been in our home for twenty-six years, except for a period when my mother requested it on extended loan.

In *Poppa Max's General Store* (p.10), Frank portrays his father, Reuben, as a workingman in suspenders and rolled sleeves, crowned with a carefully coiffed pompadour. Leaning against the shop counter, he is cocooned by the hodgepodge of practical items found in a crowded general store, the composition's charming and carefully drawn detail centered by the empty white square of his shirt. Such interpretations play a very different role from their photographic, and sometimes literal, progenitors. Here Frank filters and embellishes, eliminates the muddy tonalities of the original medium, and applies his art to memorabilia, metamorphosing documentation into personal narrative.

In recent years, Frank has merged the two media by drawing directly on photographs he reproduces on photosensitive plates. *Old Beach Days*, (p.68) combines five bathers captured on film in the twenties with another foursome drawn in behind them. Their hollow figures might be seen as either cartoon-like echoes or as eerie afterimages. In a second example of this technique titled *The Old Country* (p.69), a *carte de visite* of a prosperous looking couple, made in Vienna in the nineteenth century, is reproduced on the left half of the page. The physical details of the work—its worn edges and the imprint of the photographer's studio still visible on the lower edge—identify it as an artifact. The drawn reiterations of the couple are larger, the wife's face staring out sadly from between the other couple, her skirt flowing beyond the frame. Floating beside the card, the husband, drawn only to the bottom of his morning coat, just as we see him in the photograph, is embellished by something akin to a fool's cap and bells, his gesture echoing the keepsake as he reaches into the photograph to touch his wife. Whether or not there is a conscious message in this imagery, it is nevertheless mesmerizing and piques our curiosity about this unknown European couple. The partially distressed surface on the left of the photograph, which appears to be the result of aging, was an unintended result of the printing process. By incorporating such effects in his imagery, Frank follows one of Picasso's maxims, "I try to take advantage of accidents."

Frank has co-opted a number of wedding portraits, manipulating or interpreting them in ways that suggest he is fascinated by the ritual and the meaning of marriage. The images are often obscure, for example the *Ceremonial Jigsaw* (p.13), created by cutting the plate into parts that were separately inked, then recombined and etched. What is one to make of this marriage scene? Is this couple coming together or pulling apart? What observation or knowledge of the future might have inspired this picture? *The Bridal Canopy* (p.31) and *The Chupah* (p.32) both etching and aquatints, are later, sequential works portraying two decidedly differing representations of the Jewish marriage ceremony. Inspired by the same photograph, the first bridal couple is seen in traditional dress, formally posed beneath a free-form, ribbon-like chupah and shapes that suggest falling petals. The second husband and wife are placed forward in the frontal plane of the composition, their bridal canopy wafting from a branch as they stand waist deep in a rippled lake. With the quirky exception of the groom's black tie, they are unselfconsciously nude, calm eyes staring as if into the lenses of a camera. By juxtaposing these images: one pair cosseted and veiled in the elaborate period clothing of the Jewish rite; and the second, out of doors, partly exposed and partly immersed, but still delicately framed by the wafting chupah, they might be seen as metaphors, not only for changes in the ceremony but the evolving attitudes toward coupling.

Another male and female image–this one unrelated to a family photograph–bears a title that halts us in our tracks: *Maneater* (p.14). But this provocative description accompanies an image so enigmatically charming that it all but pushes its title off the page. The figures, etched with florid decorative line, are set against a geometric background of aquatint. Color, applied by a technique called *`a la poupée*, involves the application of several tints to the plate at the same time to create a multicolor intaglio print. The pure wackiness of the two characters with their odd accoutrements—not least of which the Napoleonic figures sprouting from the head of the young female nude—is difficult to puzzle out, but whimsy is not uncommon in Frank's inventory. Who can resist the funny Seussian fantasy of *The Mothers-in-Law* (p.15), made by the same process as *Maneater* or the jaunty *Merry Way* (p.94) and *Birthday Walk* (p.95), both etchings with watercolor that call to mind the combination of color and schematic figures of Paul Klee.

The subject of the past is ongoing in Frank's work, often on a more searing note. While a print is always completed before it is titled, the emotional kernel that has subliminally sparked the composition is often exposed. A number of these images are particularly introspective and are among his most evocative representations. *In Visions of a Past* (p.33), two looming forms crowd the page. The head of the background figure has been cropped, but meaning is conveyed by a judgmental stance. The head filling the upper left corner is the focus of the composition. From a ravaged and textured visage, vividly expressive eyes stare into the middle distance, an image of an observed scene or an image of the artist within the scene. *Memory, Still* (p.84) carries a depth of feeling similar to *Visions of a Past*, but it is stylistically dissimilar. In this instance, a head and shoulders of a single figure of black, white, and gray patterns is set against a background void. Strongly raked and disheveled hair frames the cubist face, its mood conveyed by grimly tightened lips and masterfully drawn eyes that meet our stare with bitter poignancy, reflecting its unusually direct title.

In the midst of figural, storytelling pictures, an image free as liquid, such as *D-VII* (p.66), will suddenly appear in Frank's work. Inscribed on the page with only letter and number, the complete title of this print is *Dance VII*, but without this fuller description, it might be interpreted as an abstract shape or perhaps a squid floating in an orange sea. Another dance-inspired print is a simple pattern made by drawing on layers of wet colors, the result a shimmering, translucent image called *Missed Step* (p.109). Again, the title compels the viewer to bind the image to words. If one is familiar with Frank's other dancers, *Missed Step* will resonate in its form and energy with *Step 2* (p.106). But rather than the limpid quality of *Missed Step*, *Step 2* is an example of Frank's ability to draw figures so energetic that they nearly leap from the page.

Diverse types of humor are portrayed in Frank's large body of prints, and he uses a variety of means to convey these tones. These joyful constructs result often, I think, from his delight in the modus operand of the moment. At his disposal is an array of tools and materials that can complement a mood, or spark one as he goes along. Because of his fluency in so many techniques, his bag of tricks is large. *Cantering Duo* (p.53) portrays a fanciful couple perched on a prancing steed. Against a dappled background plane, their sinuous shapes were limned with an electric graver, its skittering line affecting a sense of delicate movement. A completely different work, both stylistically and technically, *The Entertainer* (p.89), combines a ground of blue *chine collé*, on which a drawing is made by a stream of glue, the tube held delicately, like a conductor's baton, to make its lyrical form, which is then printed on the etching press.

Strong calligraphic figures play a leading role in Frank's roster of styles. Two earlier examples, *Calligraphic Woman* (p.38) and *Calligraphic Head* (p.38), have straightforward titles describing both subject and method. Small works measuring seven by five inches, they consist of black, script-like strokes printed on a rose-colored paper. Later, gestural figures such as *Pirouettes* (p.54), a sugar lift on copper, share a strongly inscriptive but more painterly feel, the luxuriant black ink seeming to sit up on the paper. Their palpable vigor is the result of hand and arm in motion. These compelling forms are combined successfully with color in a series of carborundum etchings *Sui G* (p.51), *Sylph-IV* (p.52), and *Relaxation* (p.57). Small sheets, they are sufficiently robust to communicate from a distance, but closely viewed, the softness of the torn paper, the blurred edges of the inked figures, and a subtle background made by smudging and streaking the plate, all combine to fashion diminutive, jewel-colored objects.

Recently, Frank has practiced image making that involves appropriating another artist's work—color photographs made by his wife, Naomi Feldman. By carefully selecting details from her landscape images, often choosing areas with repeated shapes, he uses them as abstract backgrounds over which he superimposes drawing and texture. The subjects are familiar: line drawings of nudes: *Figures at Bay* (p.110); imagined portraits: *Pipe with Friend* (p.121); and dance: *One Step at a Time* (p.118). By co-opting Naomi's pictures, he imbues his work with new moods, often crafting unexpected effects with light and color, like those in *Dancing Trees* (p.93).

Some subject areas, including Frank's self-portraits, the law, and his marvelous illustrated books, have not been discussed in this essay, although they are important aspects of his multi-faceted body of printed works. Having known Frank for twenty-six years, first as a mentor and later, as a friend, I think about his work in a very personal way. During this exercise, while taking license with my admittedly analytical interpretations, I have sometimes imagined Frank rising suddenly and barking in a lawyerly manner, "Conjecture!" or "Objection!" These observations and ideas are submitted with respect for the quality and inventiveness of imagery that clearly stands on its own. Added to that, however, I confess an abiding fascination with the "issues" Frank explores about life–issues so keenly expressed by his art that we recognize them in our own lives.

Janis Conner

Frank Feldman and I have worked together over a number of years. Ours has been a special collaboration; he, the creator of images on metal plates—etchings, drypoints, mezzotints—and I, the "master printer," who undertakes the responsibility of producing the most sensitive and accurate rendition of what he has envisioned. We both believe that we are "artists" in a collaborative mode and endeavoring to achieve what each of us will think, and then say: "That should do it." To collaborate with Frank is to work with a boyish investigator who never stops asking questions. Fortunately, I usually can anticipate most of the questions, and the answers to these inquiries usually satisfies both Frank's curiosity and my love of being a print technician.

Our work generally begins when Frank brings me a proof of the image that he has pulled on his press. Both of us know that this is only a starting point. My role now begins as the master printer—to be a fine-tuned human tool—to use knowledge, experience, and hopefully taste, to bring out the best in what has been tried.

The first step is for me to pull a proof which will set the standard and guide for the prints to follow. In short, to "pull the image" which will become the BAT—the *bon à tirer*—for the prints to follow, generally the signed and numbered edition. To reach that point of producing the desired visual image by manipulating ink on a matrix, certain preliminary questions need to be addressed by us: what paper and ink are to be used; is the image to have plate tone or a crisp clean wipe; are there to be special effects, such as the use of *chine collé* or *repoussage*; will there be a second or more colors, and if so, how are they to be added.

My strength as a printer is, I believe, in my versatility and willingness to expand on the traditional repertoire of techniques and to be flexible. Having an unusual bag of tricks of the trade, it is possible for me to be selfless in this collaborative process. With Frank, as with others, I am conscious of the fact that I should give my opinion generally only when asked, and to pay great respect when making a technical suggestion.

Most of the prints that I print for Frank are intaglio, meaning that the printing image is beneath the surface of the plate. This requires placing (i.e. wiping) the ink into the cuts or grooves in the plate. It also means that the pressure of the press must be adjusted so that the appropriate amount of ink is expelled under pressure. Except for approximate fifteen items in this catalog, all of the prints are in one kind of intaglio or another.

But Frank and I have also produced prints using a more intricate technique. Borrowing from the tradition of *chine collé* (which normally might use Japanese hand-made papers), Frank has used beautiful abstract nature color photographs taken by his wife and combined them with his etched image to produce images which have a uniqueness that give a different and very refreshing look. The abstract photographs, coupled with the etched image in the plate, confounds the viewer, not recognizing the precise nature of the subject.

The "collaging" technique has presented special problems, which were a challenge for me to meet. In this process the original photograph is not used. Rather, a laser copy is made of the photograph. This copy is to be used as the *chine collé*. But applying this type of copied photograph has frustrating problems. Normally, I would use methyl cellulose for the adhesion. However, I found that the use of methyl cellulose resulted in buckling of the photograph. Reviewing the range of adhesives that are available I used a dry adhesive which solved the problem; no more buckling.

Our most ambitious collaboration, and of which I am extremely proud, is our joint effort on the Alphabet Book, *When I Grow Up, A Book Person's Dream.* This book consist of illustrating, in alphabet fashion, all of the phases of making and enjoying books (such as A for Apprentice, B for Bookbinder, C for Calligrapher, etc.). Each subject is illustrated with twenty-six miniature etchings, colored by the *pochoir* process, and accompanied by text composed by Frank.

To print this edition of twenty-six copies, after the twenty-six intaglio plates were printed in black and white with oil-based printing ink, the prints were to be colored. This was to be accomplished by a technique call *pochoir* (started in France); in the United States we call it stencil printing. To learn as much as I could about the process, I went to the Museum of Modern Art print study room for three days and looked at every *pochoir* print they could pull from storage. Most impressive to me was Mastisse's book *Jazz* where all of his famous images were printed by extremely gifted French master printers. This research helped me solve some of the quirks of using the water based medium together with the oil-based printing ink. While oil and water generally do not mix, that is certainly not true with the *pochoir* process. And I believe that *When I Grow Up* is a good example of this feeling.

Regardless of the project, working with Frank has been a learning experience at every turn. After making ten or fifteen prints, the choreography would fall in place, and only nuance adjustments were necessary—wipe less, highlight some detail, keep the edges clean. Frank is a treasure at this point because he encourages me to suggest what is true to the plate and trusts that I will make choices that benefit his creation.

A word about resources: one cannot think of becoming a fine printer without having access to significant sources for the basic materials. Fortunately, in the New York area, there are some superb ones around. Some specialize in fine printing papers from all over the world; there are others for book binding supplies, archival adhesives, and letter press tools. Across the country, there are a number of suppliers who essentially deal with mail orders. Adhesives can be tricky. Methyl cellulose does not always work as desired, and often one or more dry adhesives can produce excellent results. As I tell my interns: "most of the jobs around here are handling of fine art printing paper: we choose it, tear it, wet it, print it, dry it, curate it, sign it, chop it, document it, and sell it." For that you need good resources, humans and objects.

We have also worked together together on other forms of graphic art other than intaglio. A couple of years ago, I introduced Frank to paper lithography—where one uses a Xerox paper as the plate, rather than stone or an aluminum plate. Frank was an enthusiastic student and produced some intriguing prints. When one looks at the variety of his work, one will readily see a man who likes to explore, at least in printmaking.

There are all kinds of love affairs. Some are long; many are short. One continuous one for me has been my relationship with copper plates and fine hand-made paper. The warm glow of a copper plate and its ability, after steel facing, to produce large editions with no abrasion from ink and tarlatan has provided me with unique pleasure. Having studied traditional ukeyoe printing in Japan has given me great respect for all forms of Asian papers. For a printer, there are few more sensitive moments than seeing the results of an image printed from a copper plate on fine hand made paper.

Printmaking and printing the works of fellow artists have given me great pleasure. And working with Frank has nurtured into a meaningful artist collaboration. Perhaps, there is no better comment about printing and collaborating than the statement of Julio Valdez: " We must learn to honor the thinking and the feeling of the medium in order to penetrate the poetry of it (and)... learn the temperament of the technique." Frank and I have tried to accomplish this.

Kathy Caraccio

Introductory Note

All of the prints are intaglio, except for twelve transfer prints and four limited edition books.

All of the intaglio prints are in an edition size of thirty, except for *Grandpa in a Tree* (p. 8), which is in an edition of seventy-five. There are also proofs of each image, which generally do not exceed five.

Some of the intaglio prints have either *chine collé* or a transferred photographic image combined with the plate. In such cases, the *chine collé* print or the transferred photographic image may be unique to the plate. In such cases, the completed print is a unique print.

The dimensions of the prints are in inches; height precedes width.

The twelve transfer prints are unique, and are comparable to monotypes or paintings with mixed media

This catalog is limited to a selection of one hundred fifty intaglio prints, transfer prints, and books. However over the period covered, there has been executed more than seven hundred fifty intaglio plates and hundreds of other prints using various forms of graphic art, such as lithography, woodcuts, wood engravings, linoleum cuts, silk screens, monotypes, collographs, and paper cutouts. In the last fifteen years, more than a dozen limited edition books using multiple forms of printmaking techniques have been produced.

Copies of the prints and books have been acquired by a number of public rare book and print collections, including The New York Public Library (Print Division and Dance Collection of the Performing Arts), The University of Texas at El Paso (Rare Book Library), Harvard University (The Houghton Library), Yale University (Sterling Memorial Library), Columbia University (Rare Book Library), Brown University (John Hay Library), Princeton University (Rare Book Library), The Jewish Theological Seminary of America, Hebrew University College, Portland Art Museum (Lynd Ward Memorial Collection), and the British Museum (Department of Prints and Drawings).

FF

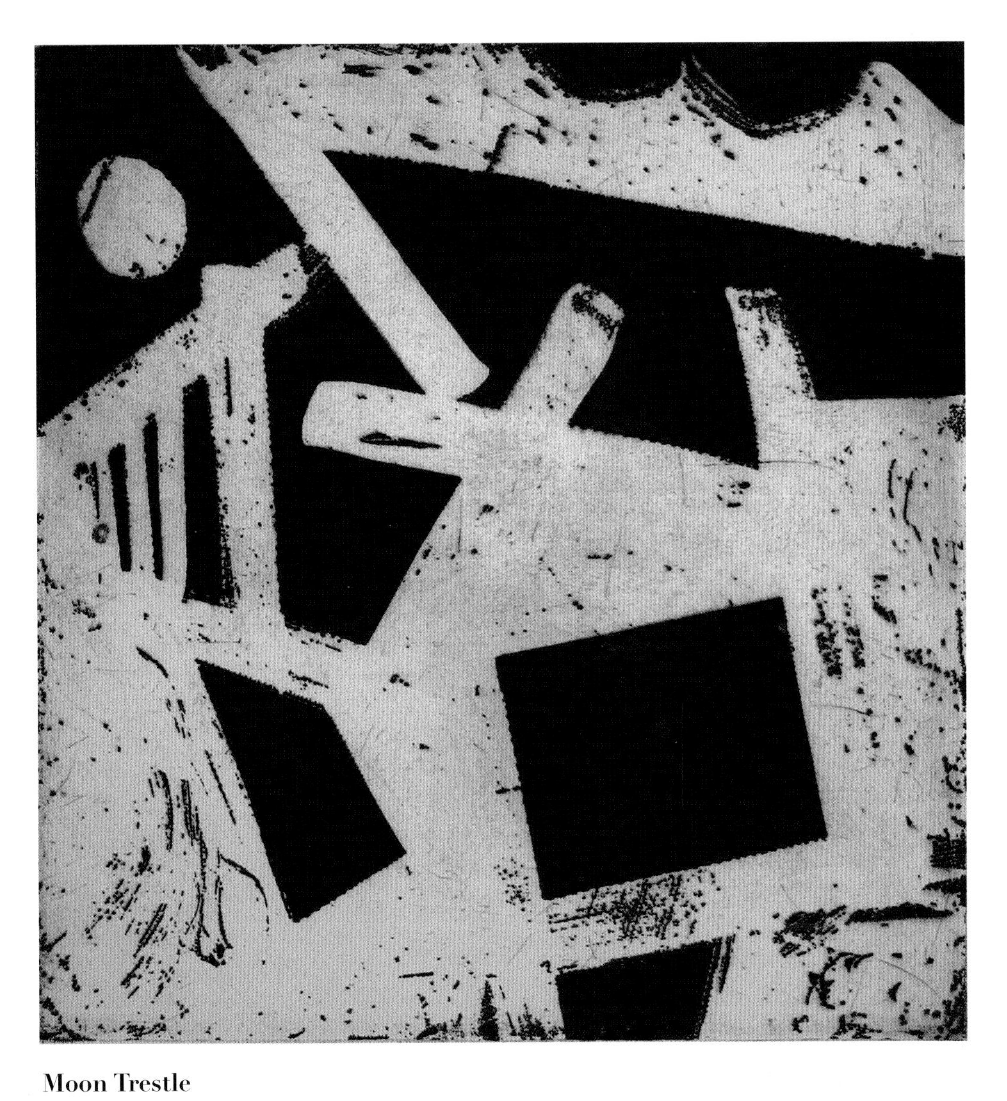

Moon Trestle

(1969) etching with aquatint,
8 7/8 x 9

Moon, Hat, and Bosom

(1969) etching,
6 x 6

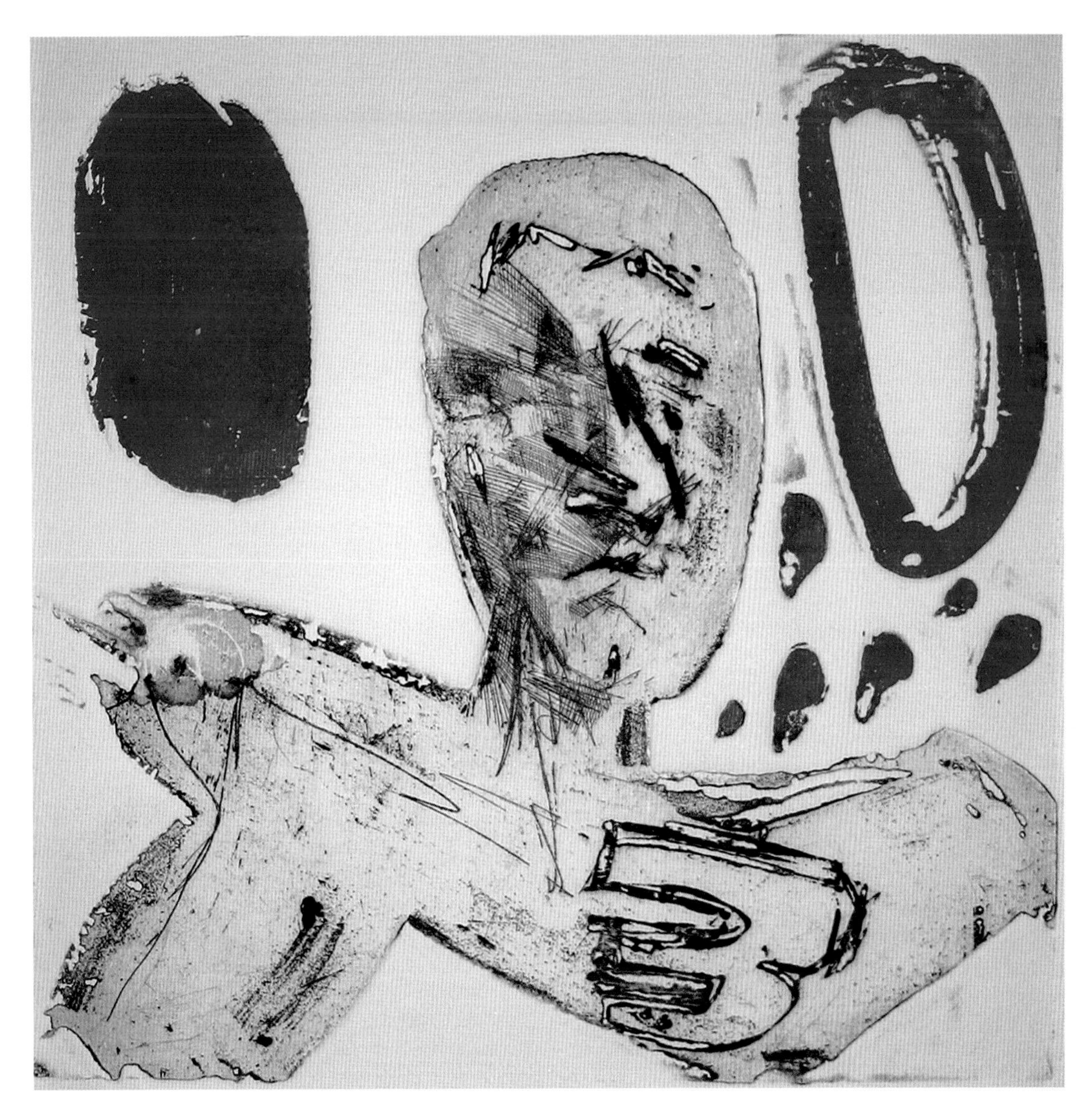

The Football Player

(1969) etching,
8 7/8 x 9

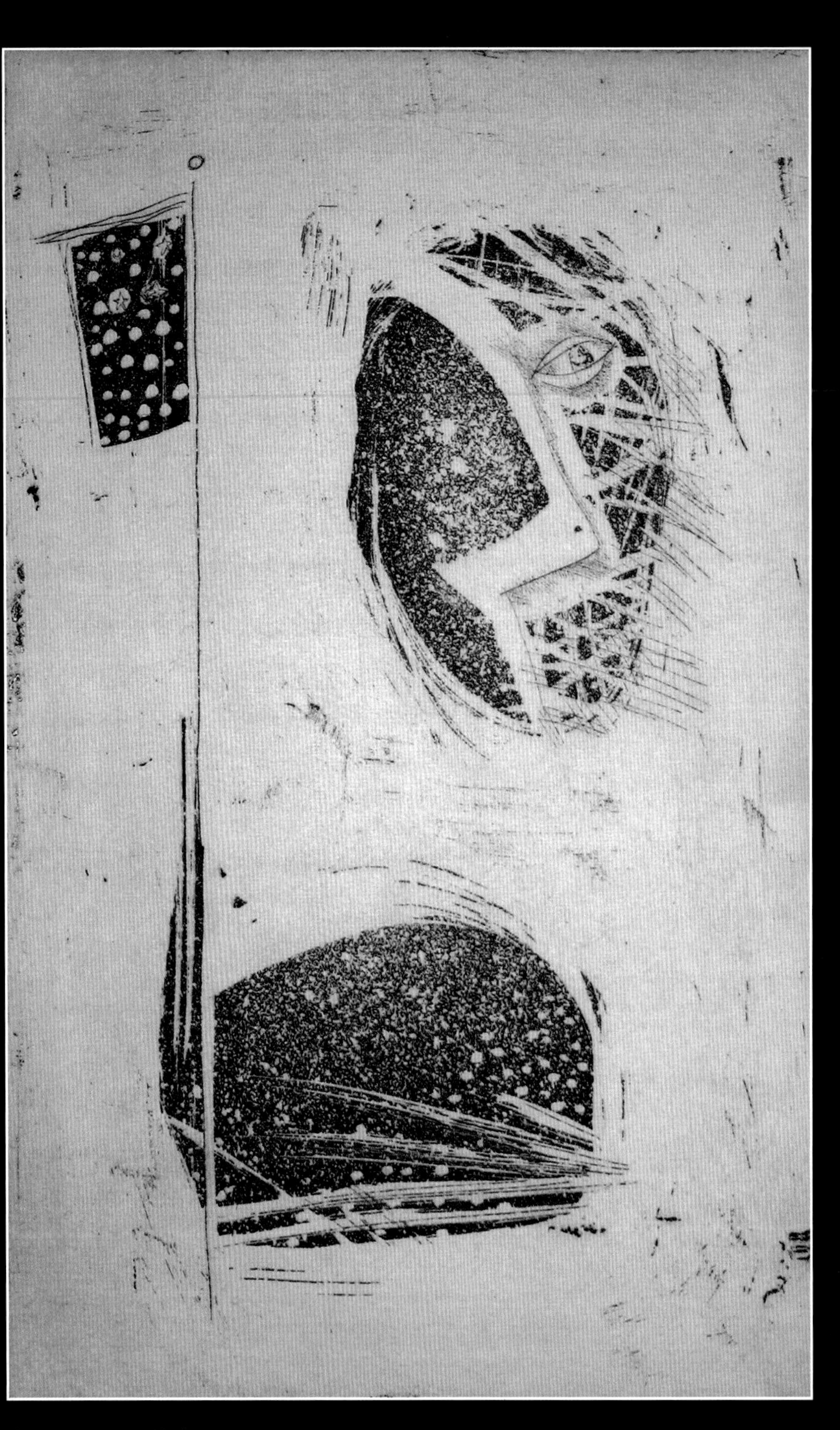

Conscientious Believer

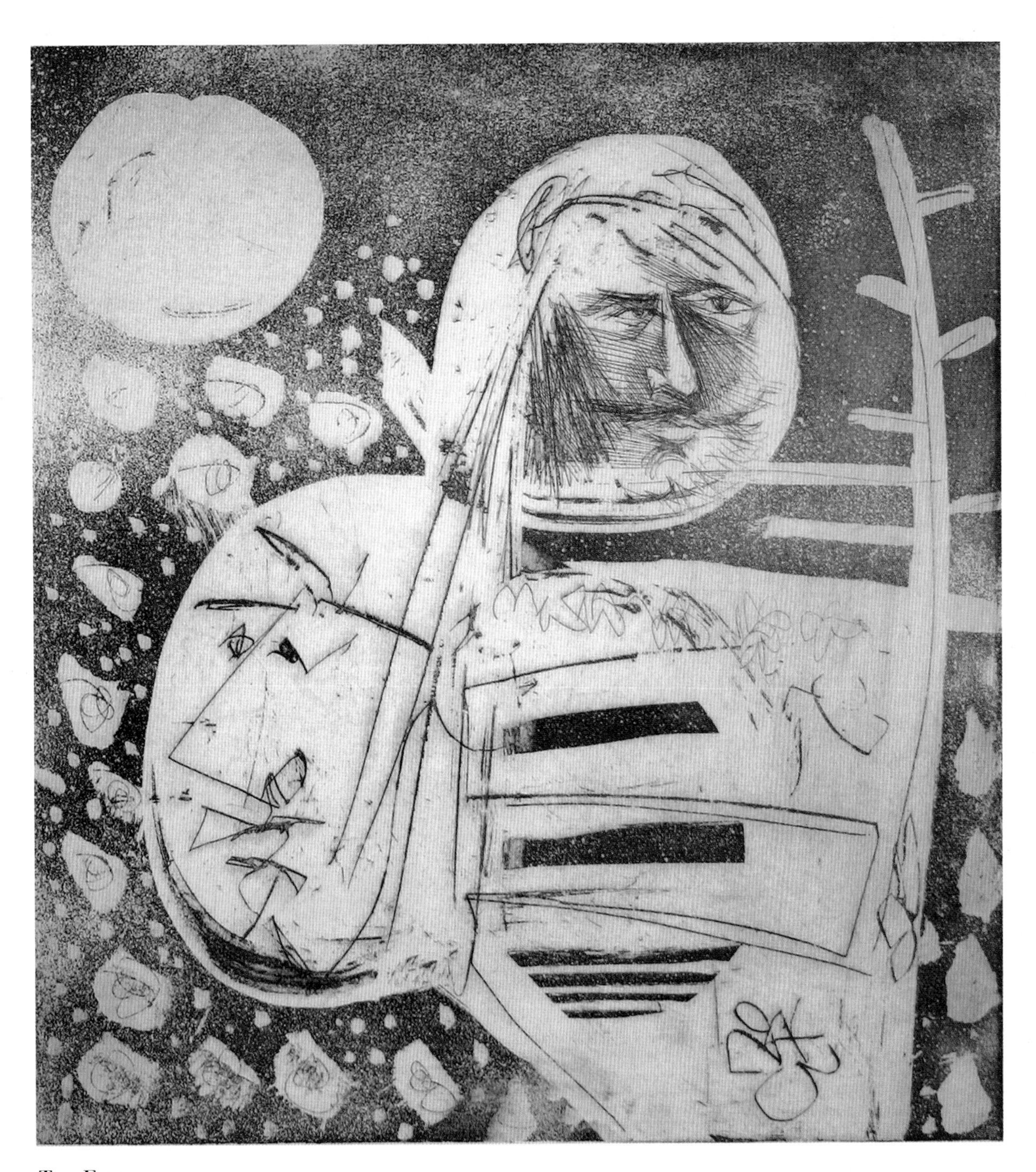

Two Faces

(1970) etching with aquatint,
9 9/16 x 8 7/8

Grandpa in a Tree

(1970) etching with aquatint,
12 x 10

The Wedding Party

(1970) etching with aquatint,
8 1/4 x 9

Poppa Max's General Store

(1971) etching,
12 x 12

Fish Story

(1971 etching with aquatint
and photogravure,
14 x 12

Head and Shoulder

(1971) etching with aquatint,
6 1/4 x 4 1/2

Ceremonial Jig Saw

(1972) etching with aquatint,
10 x 6 1/2

Maneater

(1972) etching with aquatint,
9 3/4 x 9 3/8

The Incumbent

(1972) etching,
5 3/8 x 4 1/2

The Mothers- in- Law

(1972) etching with aquatint,
9 x 8 1/8

Images of Dad

(1972) etching with aquatint
and photogravure,
8 x 6 13/16

Two Sisters

(1972) etching with aquatint,
4 1/2 x 4 7/16

Family Portrait

(1972) etching with aquatint,
diameter 5

Al and Reubie

(1973-74) etching with aquatint,
diameter 5

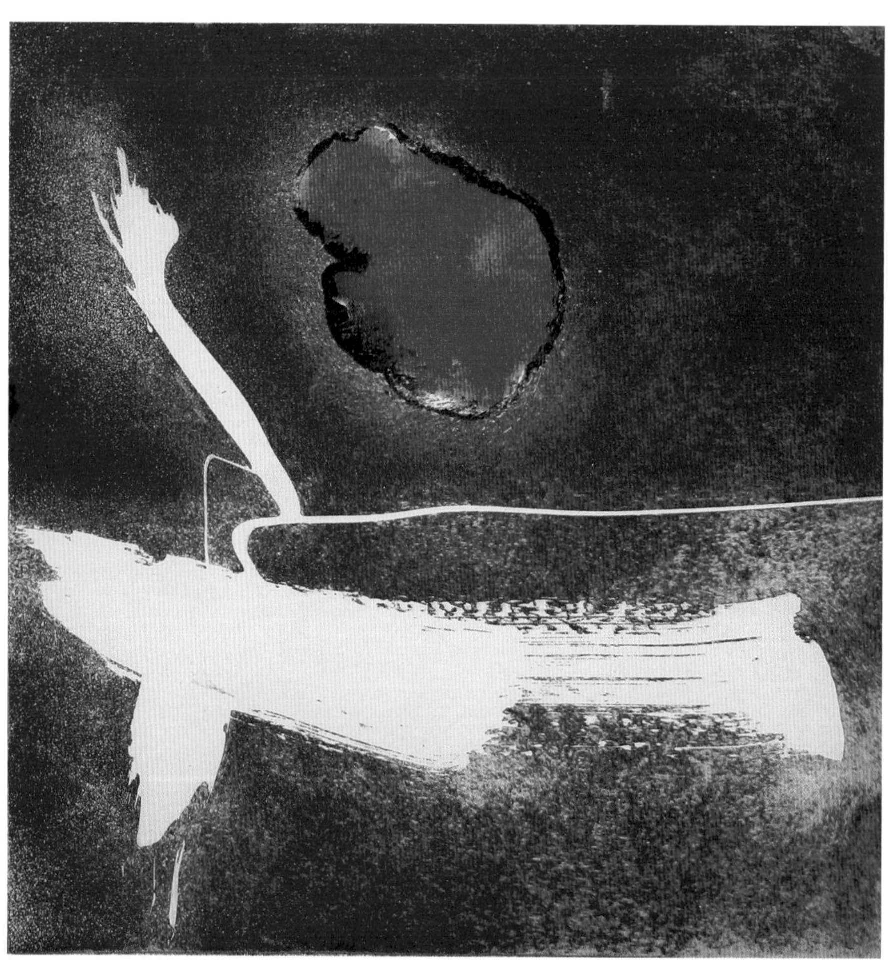

Rotary Saucer

(1973) etching with aquatint,
8 7/8 x 9

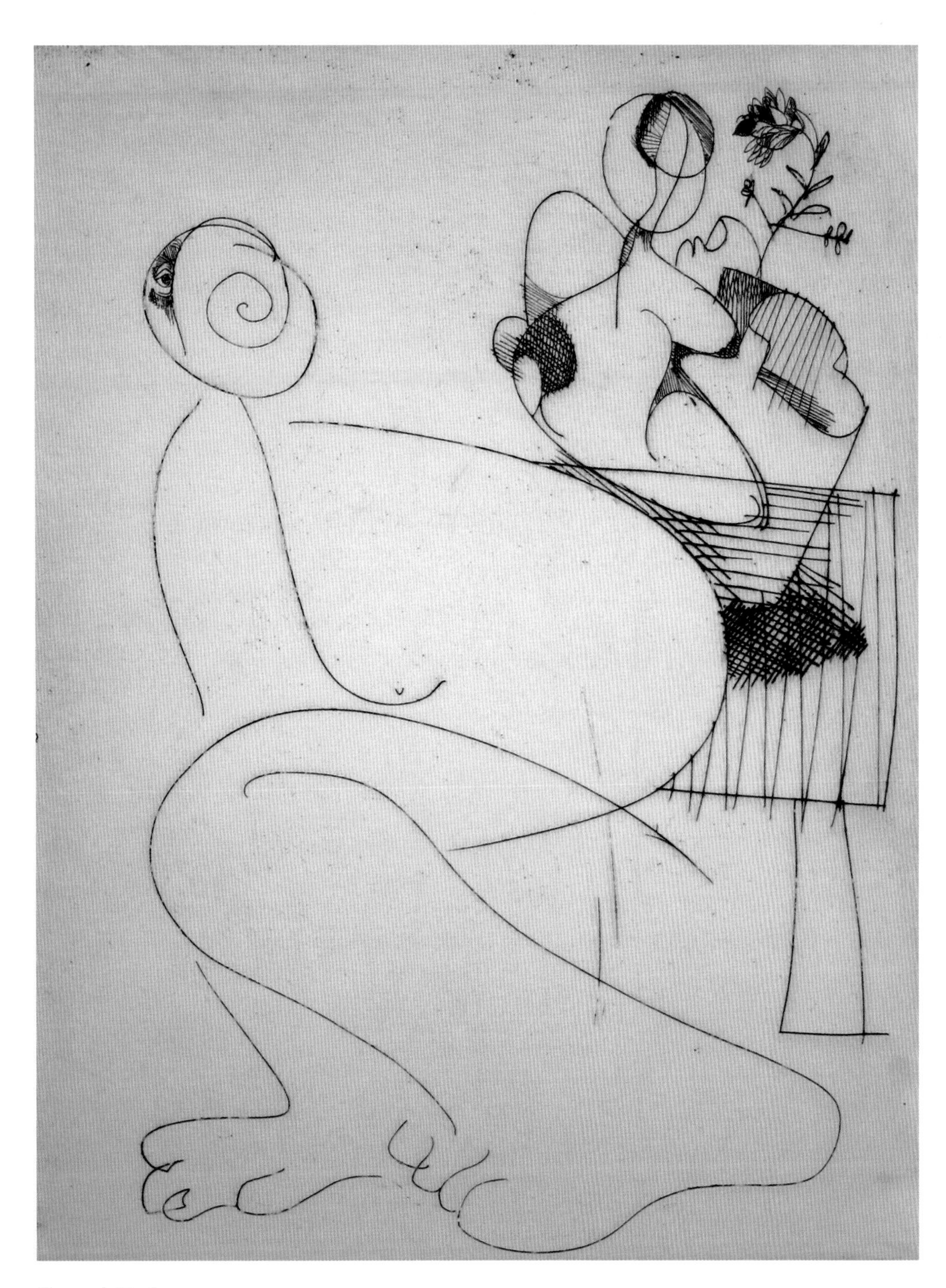

Seated Nude

(1974) etching,
12 x 9

Self-P, as Young B-

(1974) sugar lift ground etching,
4 1/2 x 4 3/8

Daddy and Me

(1975) etching with electric graver,
diameter 6

Irving, Hold It! The Survey is Not Right

(1975) etching with aquatint,
8 1/8 x 8 15/16

The Workshop

(1975) etching,
9 x 8

Press Me Fondly

(1975) etching with aquatint,
11 1/8 x 8 5/8

The Atelier

(1976) etching with aquatint,
4 1/2 x 4 1/2

Justice-III

(1976) etching,
12 3/4 x 8 13/16

Justice-IV

(1977) rolled etching.
9 7/16 x 8 9/16

You, Claudius

(1978) etching,
11 3/4 x 9 11/16

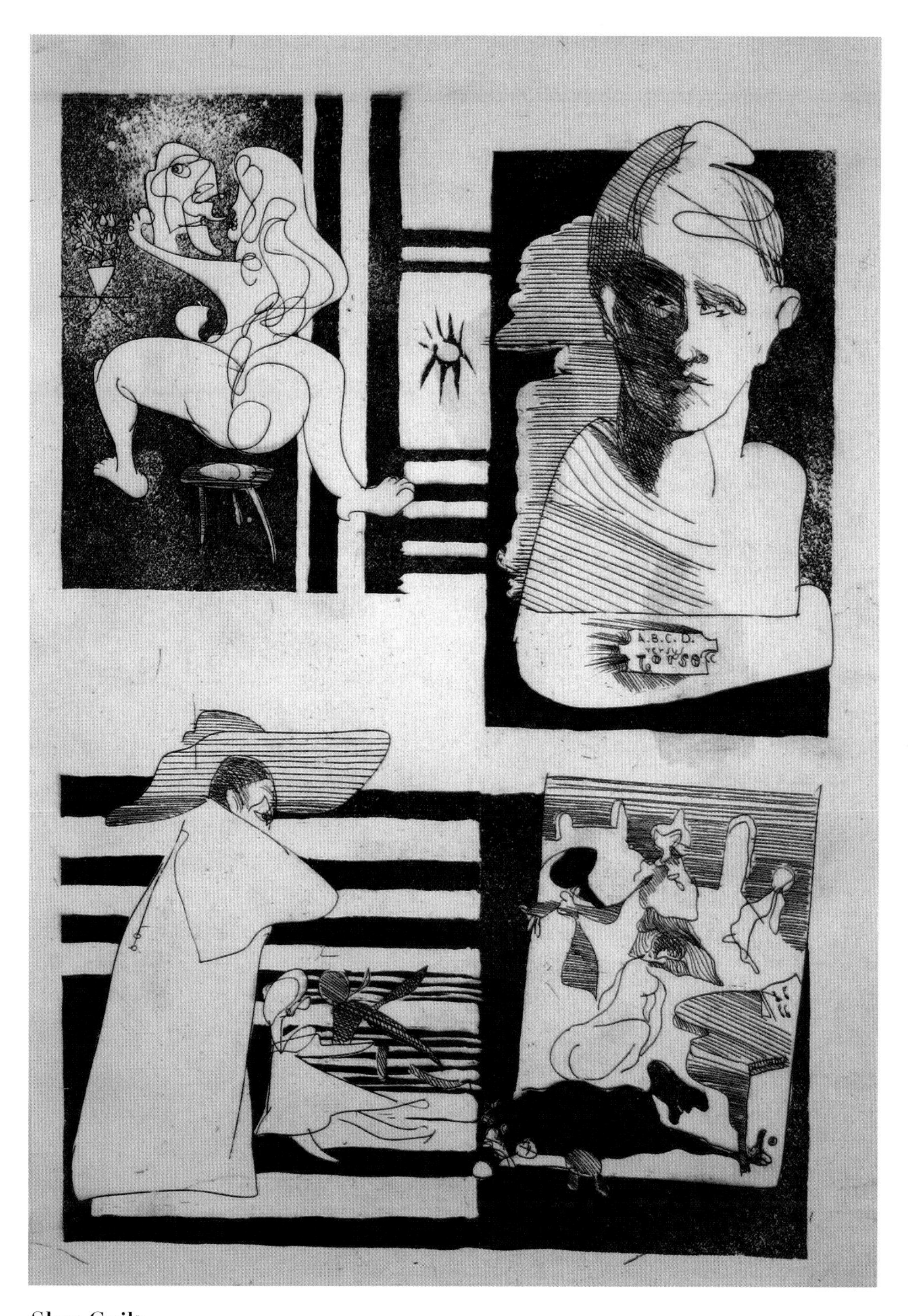

Slow Guilt

(1978) etching with aquatint.
13 1/4 x 8 7/8

After the Beginning

(1978) etching,
8 3/4 x 8 3/4

Metamorphosis

(1978) etching with aquatint,
8 3/4 x 8 3/4

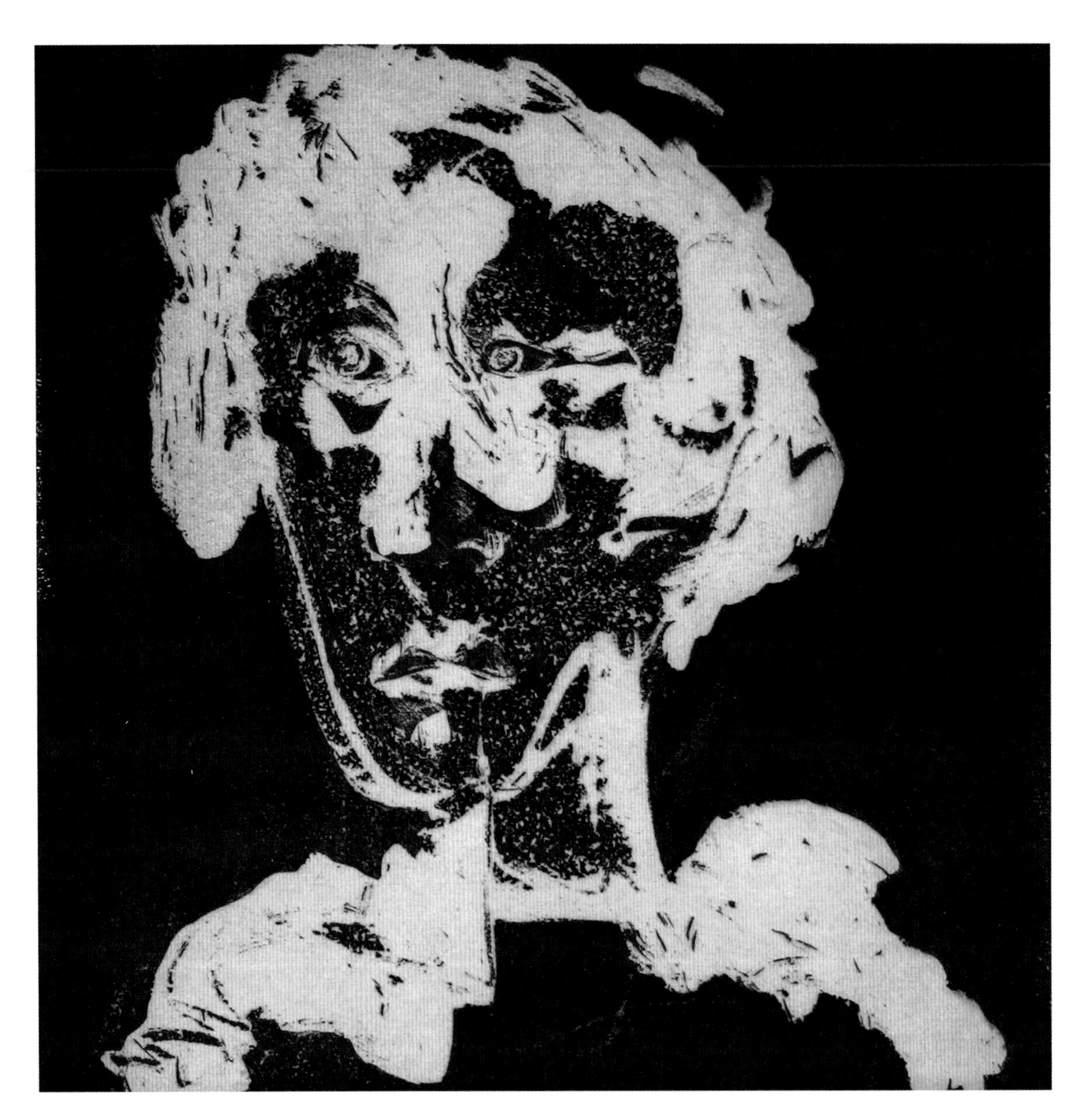

Young Man

(1978) etching with aquatint,
8 13/16 x 8 13/16

The Bridal Canopy

(1978) etching with aquatint,
9 7/8 x 6 1/4

The Chupah

(1978) etching with aquatint,
8 3/4 x 8 7/8

Visions of a Past

(1979) etching with aquatint,
8 15/16 x 11 3/4

The Joys of Justice Runneth Over

(1979) etching with aquatint,
8 7/8 x 17 11/16

It Doesn't Please His Honor

(1979) etching,
11 7/8 x 11 7/8

We Found Her

(1980) etching with aquatint,
8 7/8 x 8 15/16

Still Life With Model

(1980) etching,
8 11/16 x 8 15/16

Pastoral

(1980) etching with aquatint
and relief roll,
6 7/8 x 9

Calligraphic Woman

(1981) etching with *chine collé*,
7 x 4 15/16

Calligraphhead

(1981) etching with *chine collé*,
6 15/16 x 4 7/8

Quick Learner

(1982) etching with aquatint,
11 3/4 x 8 15/16

Retreat

(1983) etching with aquatint,
2 x 2

Prayer Meeting

(1987) drypoint with hand coloring,
2 x 2

Dancers

(1987) mezzotint,
2 x 2

Good Friends

(1987) mezzotint,
2 x 2

F.F.

(1984) etching with aquatint,
2 x 2

Carla

(1984) etching,
6 7/8 x 4 7/8

Emily

(1984) etching,
6 7/8 x 4 7/8

Joan

(1984) etching,
6 7/8 x 4 7/8

Betrothed

(1988) mezzotint,
2 13/16 x 2 3/4

Call from the Mountain,

(1987-88) etching with aquatint,
2 x 2

The Return

(1988) mezzotint,
2 3/4 x 2 13/16

Harem

(1988) mezzotint,
2 13/16 x 2 3/4

Ensemble

(1989) etching with *chine collé*,
6 15/16 x 4 15/16

Oenophile

(1989) etching with aquatint
and *chine collé*,
6 15/16 x 4 15/16

Eric et Enide

(1989) carborundum etching
with *chine collé*,
14 7/8 x 9 15/16

Erato

(1989) carborundum etching
with *chine collé*,
14 7/8 x 9 15/16

Eye-Figure

(1989) carborundum etching
with *chine collé*,
14 7/8 x 9 13/16

Empty Hat

(1989) carborundum etching
with *chine collé*,
14 13/16 x 9 3/4

The Snob

(1990) drypoint,
9 15 /16 x 7 15/16

Sylph

(1990) carborundum etching
with *chine collé*,
6 15/16 x 4 15/16

Sui G

(1990) carborundum etching
with *chine collé*,
6 15/16 x 4 15/16

Sylph-IV

(1990) carborundum etching
with *chine collé*,
7 9/16 x 4 15/16

Cantering Duo

(1990) etching with electric
graver and aquatint,
7 15/16 x 9 7/8

Pirouettes

(1990) sugar lift ground etching,
10 x 7 15/16

Portrait of A

(1990) carborundum etching
with *chine collé.*
6 15/16 x 4 15/16

Catenary

(1990) carborundum etching
with *chine collé*,
9 15/16 x 4

Relaxation

(1991) carborundum etching
with *chine collé*,
4 15/16 x 6 15/16

KS-12

(1991) etching with aquatint,
5 1/4 x 5 7/8

Seashore

(1992) sugar lift etching
with *chine collé*,
7 15/16 x 9 13/16

The Adolescent

(1993) lithographic crayon
etching with aquatint.
6 15/16 x 5 5/16

Cynic

(1993) etching with electric
graver and aquatint,
11 7/8 x 8 15/16

Portrait Lady

(1993) lithographic crayon etching
with aquatint and hand coloring,
11 5/16 x 9

Dance-A

(1994) etching with aquatint,
11 13/16 x 8 15/16

Dance-B

(1994) etching with aquatint,
11 7/8 x 8 7/8

Dance-D

(1994) etching with aquatint,
11 15/16 x 8 7/8

D-VII

(1995) lithographic crayon
with aquatint,
3 15/16 x 3 1/4

D-VIII

(1995) lithographic crayon
with aquatint,
3 7/16 x 2 3/4

Solo 3-B

(1995) etching with aquatint
and *chine collé.*
6 7/8 x 4 3/4

Doctrine James

(1996) etching on photo-
sensitive polymer plate,
10 x 8 7/16

Old Beach Days

(1996) etching combined with photographic image on photo-sensitive polymer plate, 7 1/2 x 6 1/16

The Old Country

(1996) etching combined with photographic image on photo-sensitive polymer plate, 10 11/16 x 9 1/4

Respond After Me

(1996) etching with aquatint
combined with photographic image,
8 7/8 x 11 7/8

Viola Player

(1996) etching with
hand coloring,
3 1/2 x 2 7/8

Eleven Fifteen A.M

(1997) etching on photo-sensitive polymer plate, 10 5/8 x 7 7/8

Good Friend

(1997) sugar lift etching
with *chine collé.*
10 15/16 x 8 7/8

Dancers `a Trois

(1997-98) sugar lift etching
with *chine collé*,
4 x 5 3/4

Four Steps

(1997) sugar lift etching
with *chine collé*,
10 15/16 x 8 7/8

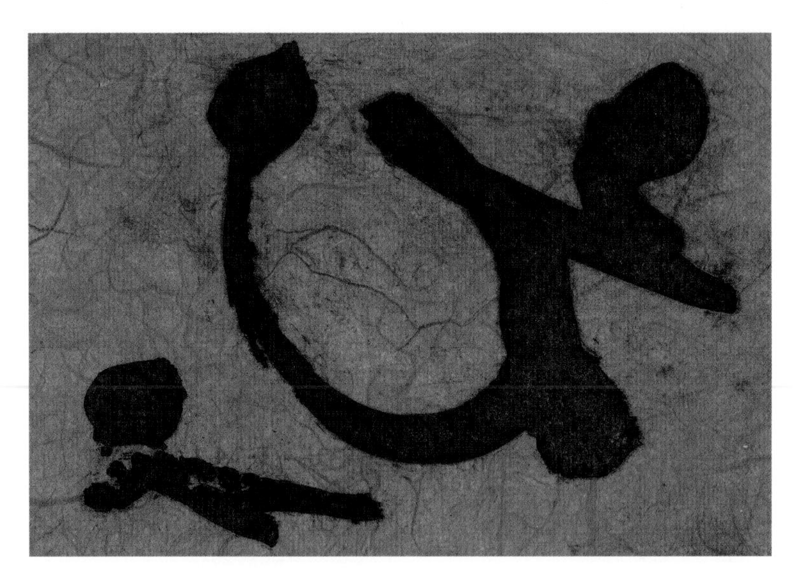

Jester

(1997-98) sugar lift etching
with *chine collé*,
4 x 5 3/4

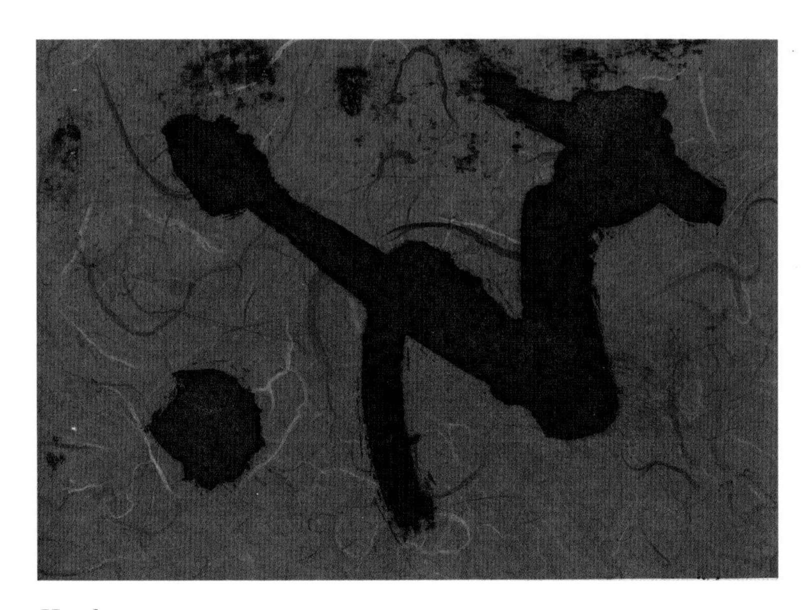

Headstrong

(1997-98) sugar lift etching
with *chine collé*,
4 x 5 3/4

Running Landscape

(1998) sugar lift etching
with *chine collé*,
4 7/8 x 7

Morgy

(1998) mezzotint,
2 15/16 x 4 1/8

Young Woman

(1998) sugar lift etching
with *chine collé*,
7 x 4 7/8

Play Time

(1998) sugar lift etching
with *chine collé*,
6 15/16 x 4 7/8

Winter Trees

(1998), sugar lift etching
with *chine collé*,
4 15/16 x 6 15/16

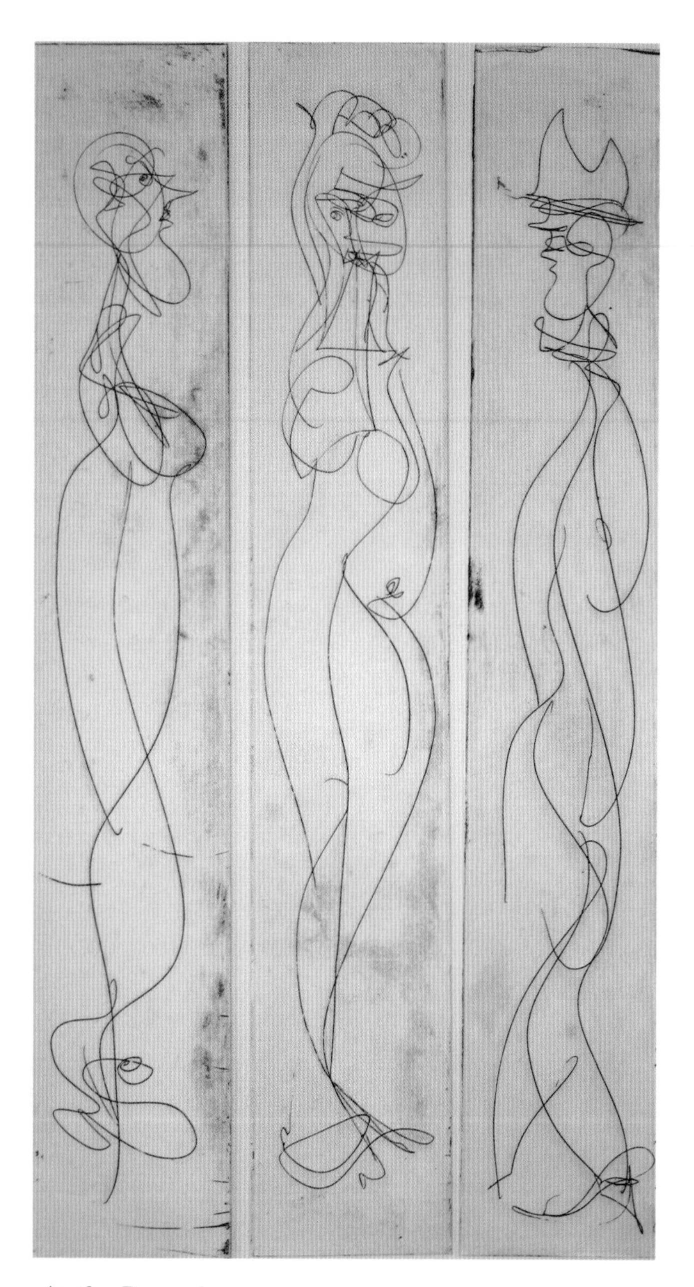

At the Reception

(1998) etching
(1st state),
10 15/16 x 6 5/16

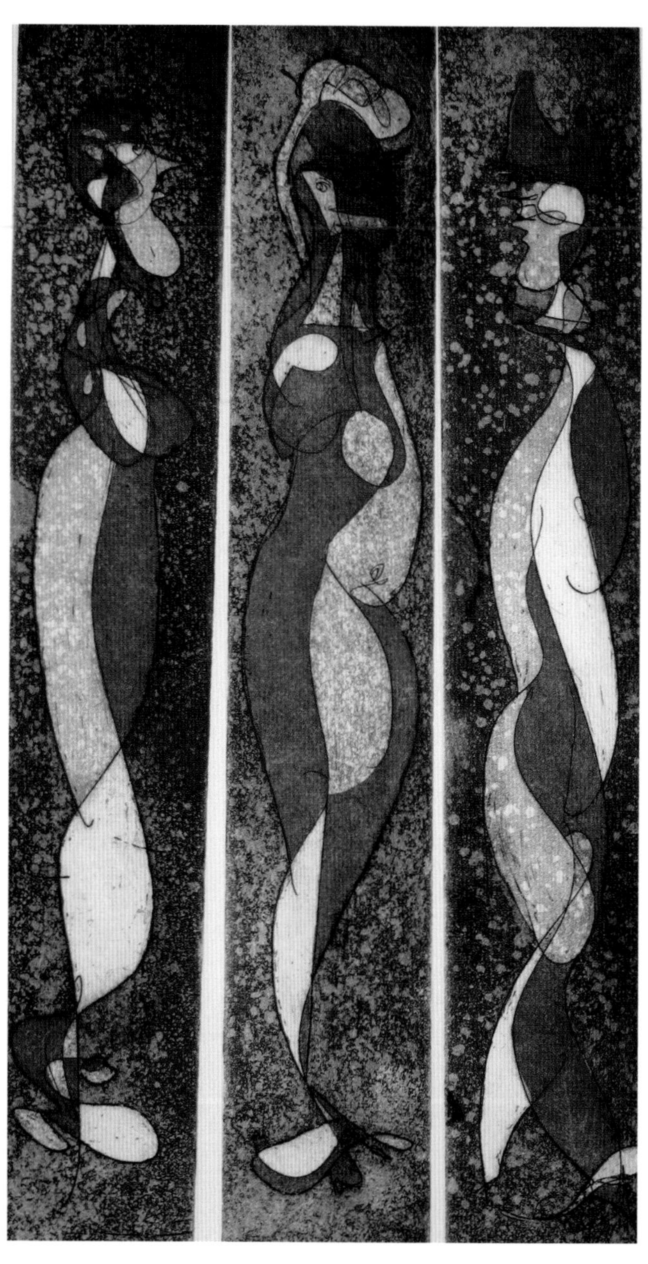

At the Reception

(1998) etching with
aquatint (final state),
10 15/16 x 6 5/16

Evening Dance

(1998) mezzotint,
4 11/16 x 5 13/16

Memory, Still

(1998) etching with aquatint,
6 15/16 x 4 15/16

Friends at the Beach

(1999) etching with aquatint,
3 x 13 7/8

FF

(1999) sugar lift etching,
10 7/8 x 8 7/8

Moving Along-II

(1999) sugar lift etching
with aquatint and photo offset,
10 7/8 x 8 13/16

Lost Tree

(1999) etching with *chine collé*,
3 1/2 x 2 15/16

Wondrous Thoughts

(1999) etching with *chine collé*,
10 7/8 x 8 7/8

Star Meets Director

(2001) carborundum etching
with *chine collé*,
11 7/8 x 8 15/16

The Entertainer

(2001) carborundum etching
with *chine collé*,
9 3/4 x 9

The Producer

(2001) carborundum etching
with *chine collé*,
11 3/4 x 8 3/4

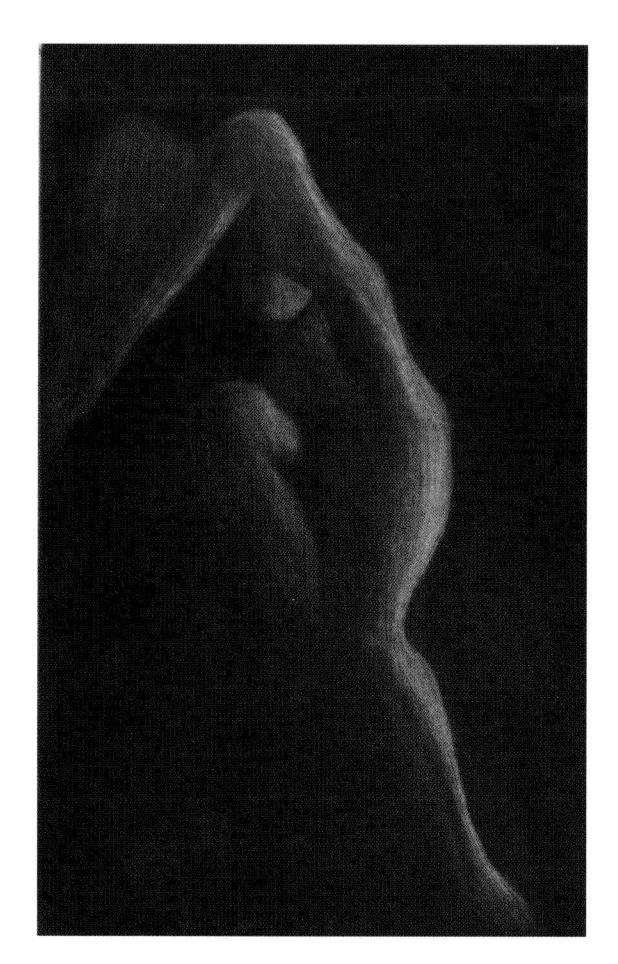

Thoughtful Nude

(2000) mezzotint,
4 5/8 x 2 15/16

Ingenue

(2001) carborundum etching
with *chine collé*,
11 7/8 x 8 15/16

Star Gazer

(2001) carborundum
etching with *chine collé*,
12 x 9

Dancing Trees

(2001) etching
with *chine collé*,
10 11/16 x 8 3/4

Merry Way

(2001) etching
with hand coloring,
2 3/16 x 8 7/8

Reverie-II

(2001) carborundum etching
with *chine collé*,
12 x 9

Birthday Walk

(2001) etching
with hand coloring,
1 3/4 x 8 3/4

Le Maitre

(2001) carborundum etching
with *chine collé*,
9 x 6

Leaf Romance

(2001) mezzotint,
5 7/8 x 4 3/4

Welcome Home

(2002) mezzotint,
5 3/4 x 8 11/16

Young Ladies

(2002) etching on polymer plate,
9 7/8 x 7 1/16

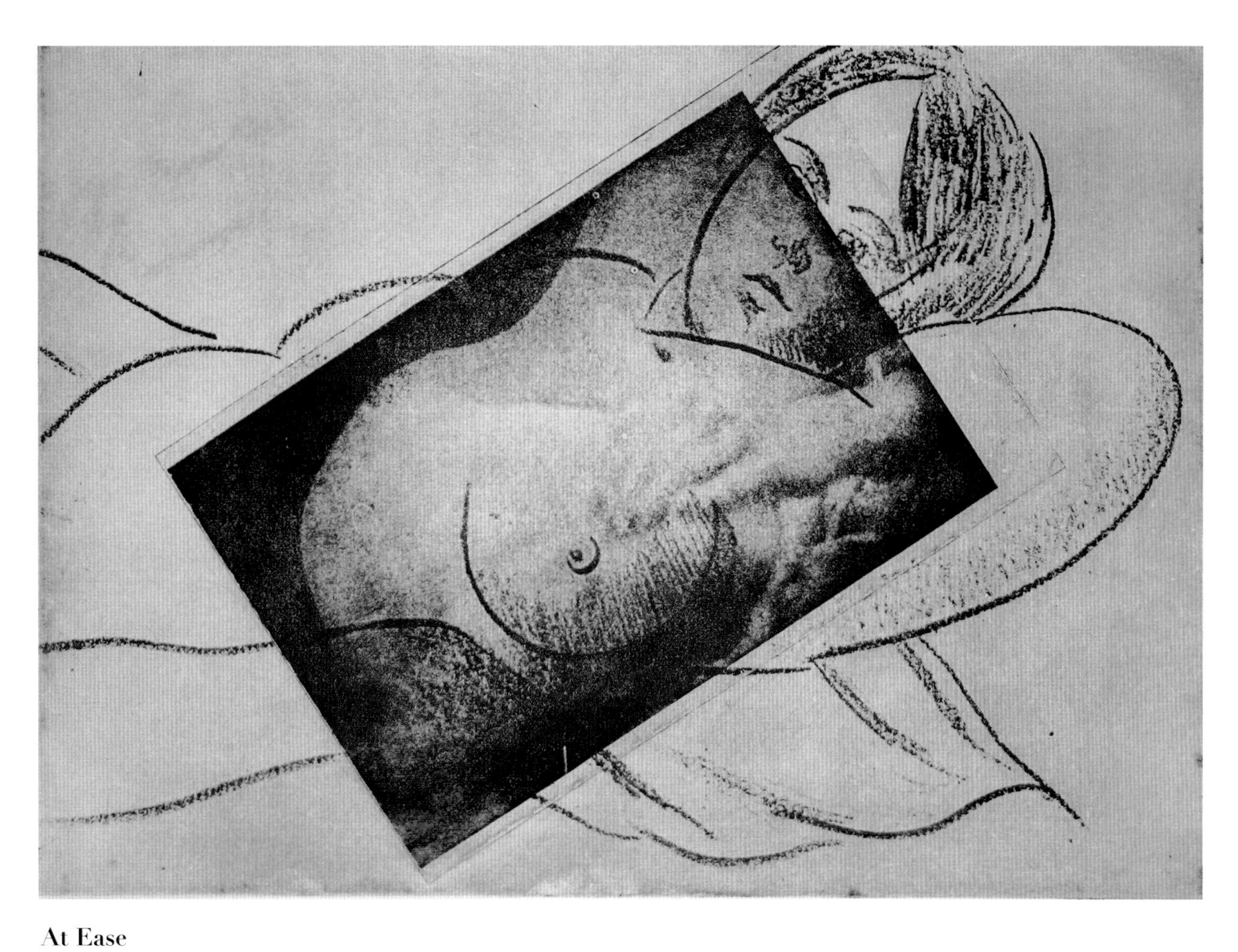

At Ease

(2002) etching on polymer plate
with photo offset,
7 x 9 7/8

Nocturne

(2002) mezzotint,
5 3/4 x 4 3/4

Finale

(2003) etching on polymer plate
with *chine collé* and photo offset,
9 7/8 x 7 7/8

Relaxation

(2003) etching with spit bite
and aquatint,
10 11/16 x 8 7/8

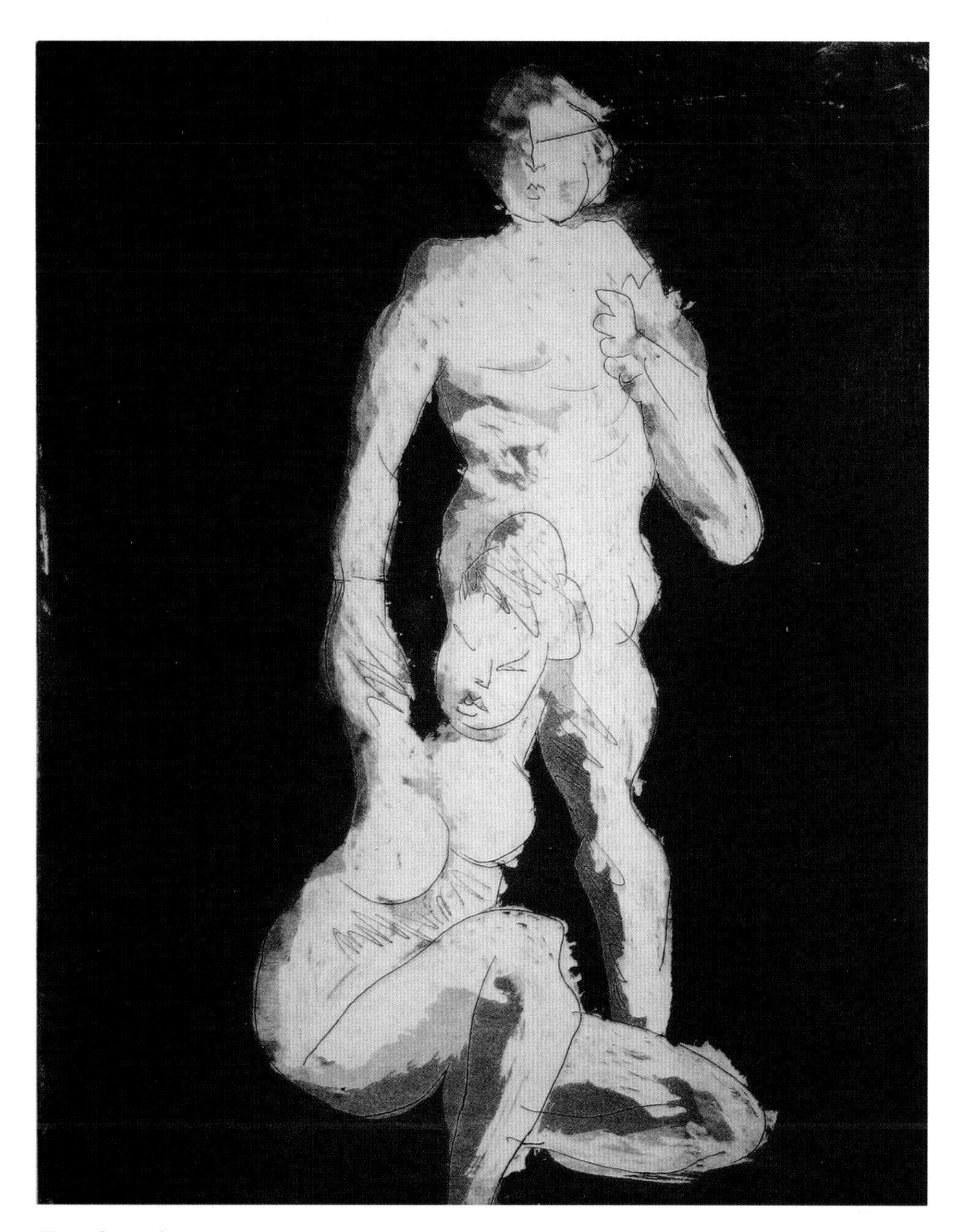

Together, Again

(2003) etching with
spit bite and aquatint,
10 11/16 x 8 7/8

Tic Tac Toe

(2003) sugar lift etching,
10 3/4 x 8 7/8

Beach Time

(2003) etching with drypoint
and aquatint,
8 7/8 x 10 13/16

Step 2

(2003) etching on polymer plate
with hand coloring,
7 x 5

Step 1

(2003) etching on polymer plate
with hand coloring,
7 x 5

Anna

(2003) carborundum etching,
6 15/16 x 7 7/8

Missed Step

(2004) etching on polymer plate
with *chine collé*,
7 x 5

Figures at Bay

(1999) transfer print,
13 1/2 x 9 3/4

Galloping Figures

(2003) transfer print,
15 x 11 1/8

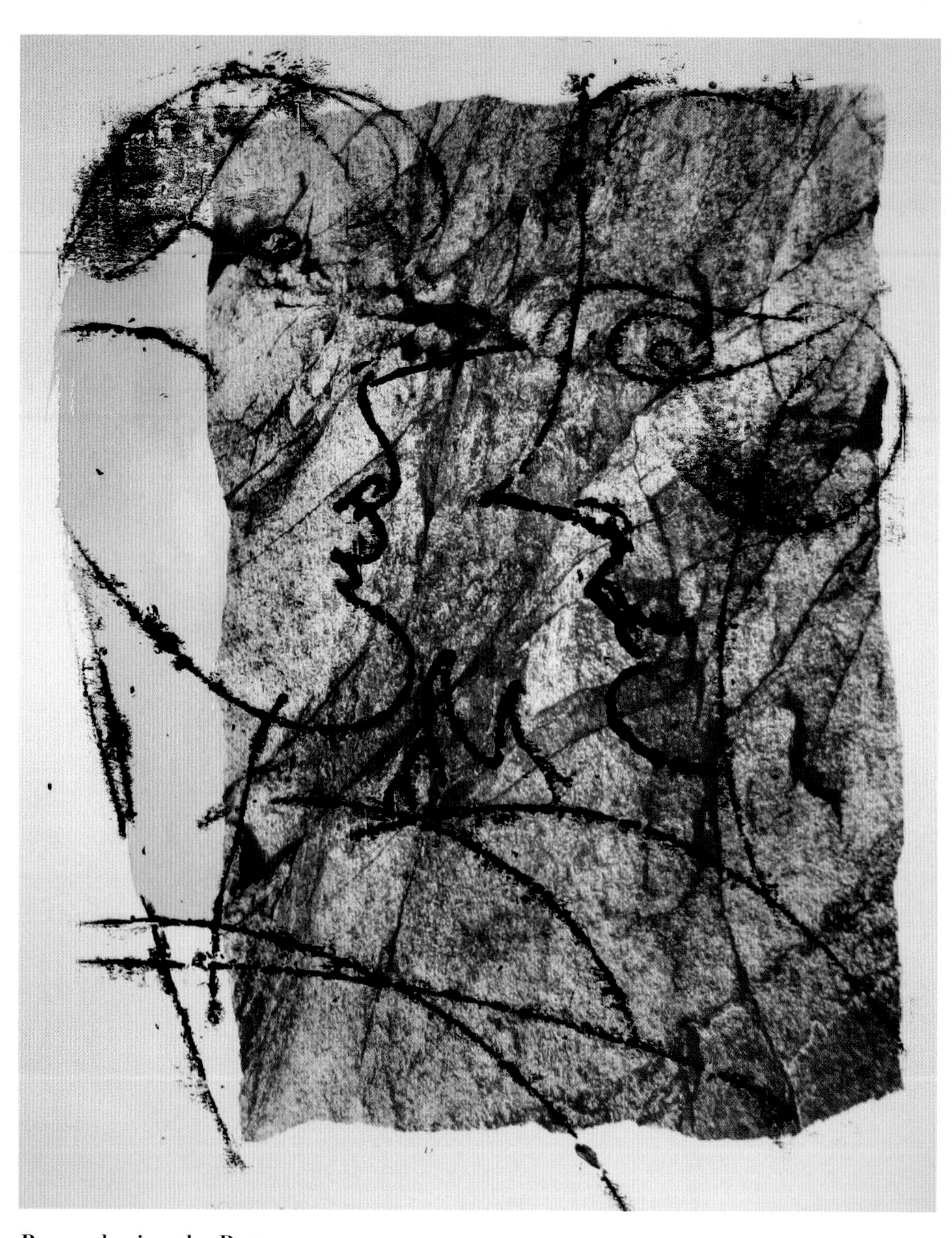

Remembering the Past

(2004) transfer print,
12 1/4 x 9 1/2

Friendly Encounter

(2004) transfer print,
13 1/4 x 10 1/2

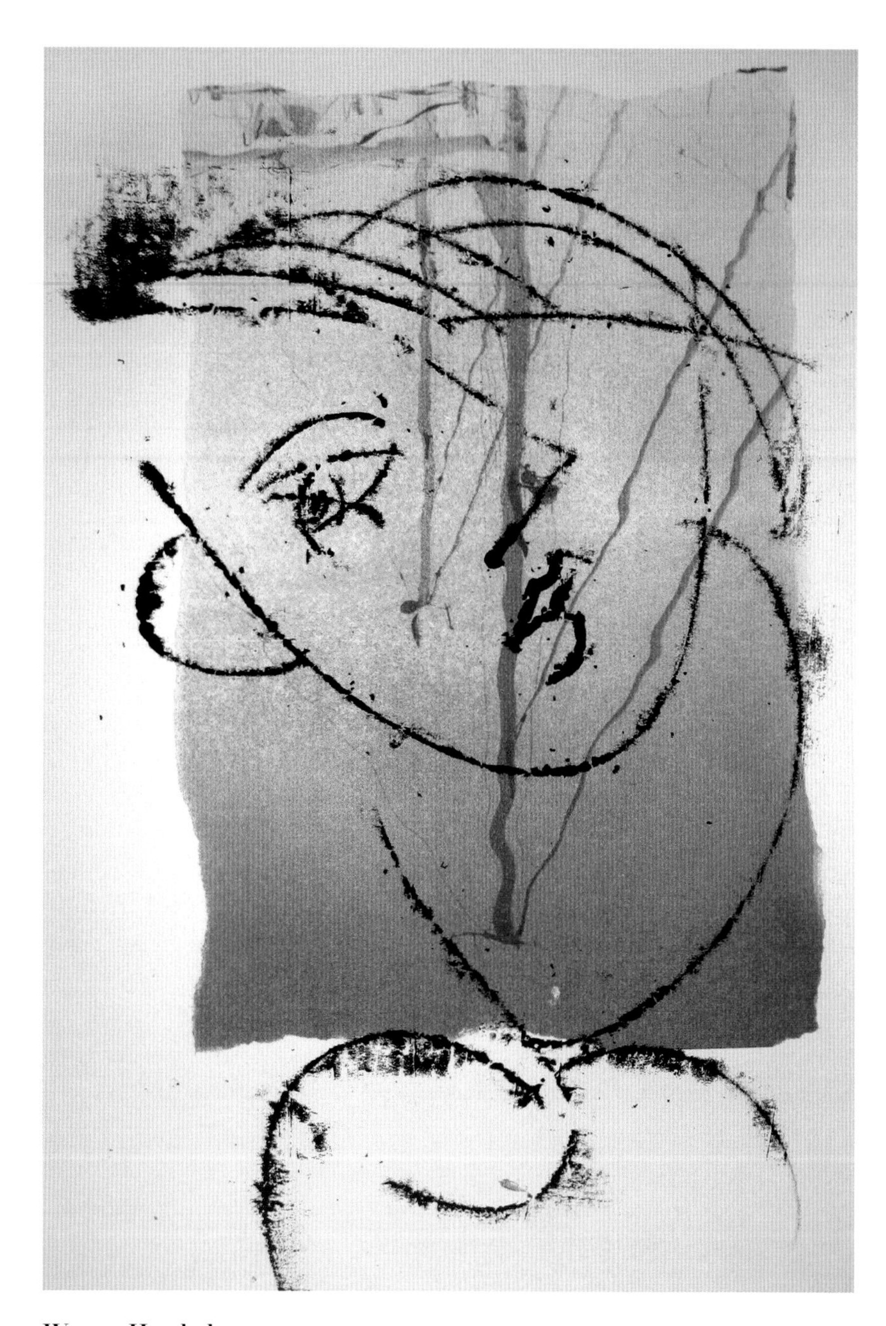

Wrong Headed

(2004) transfer print,
14 1/2 x 9 1/4

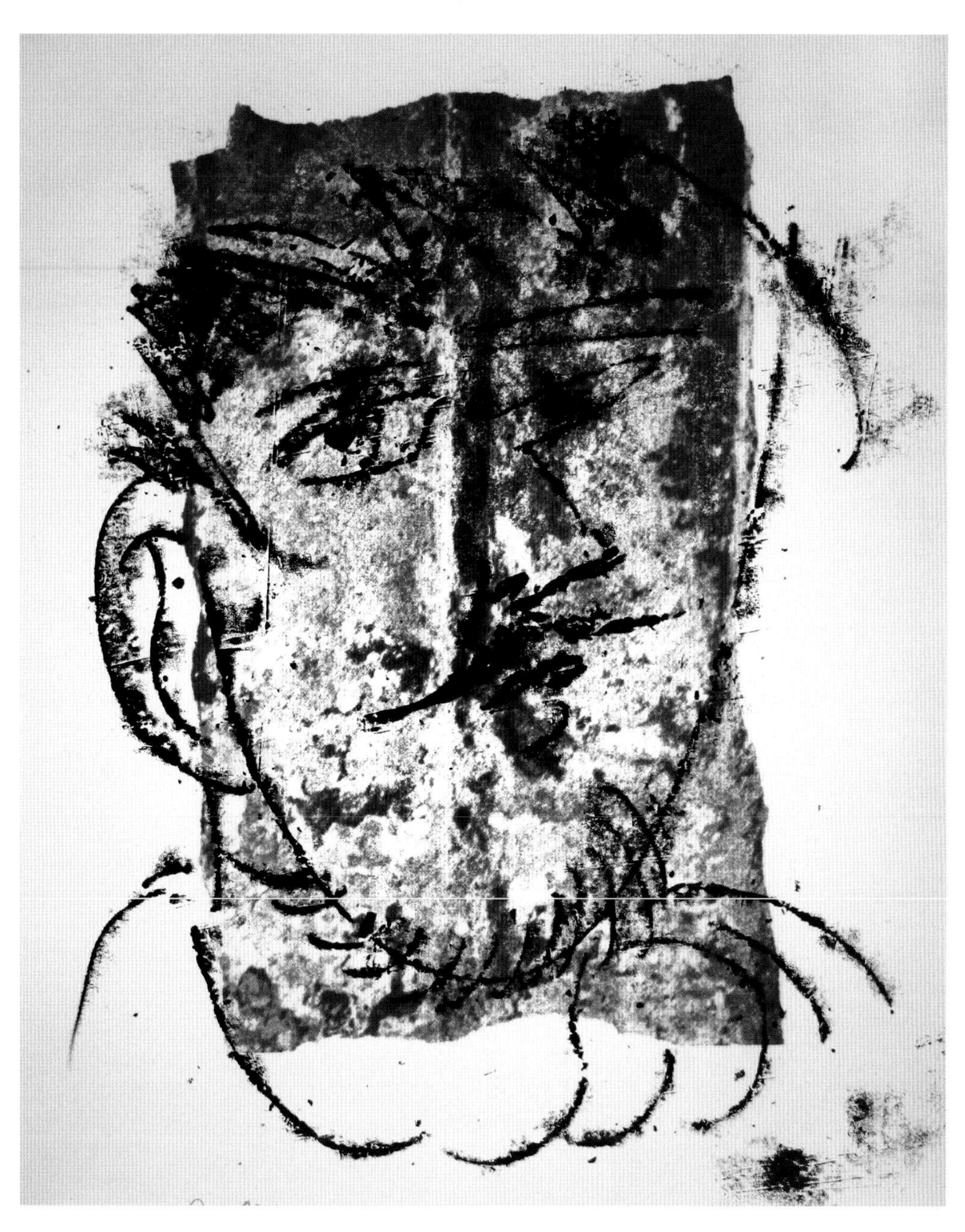

Artist at Bay

(2004) transfer print,
13 1/4 x 9 1/4

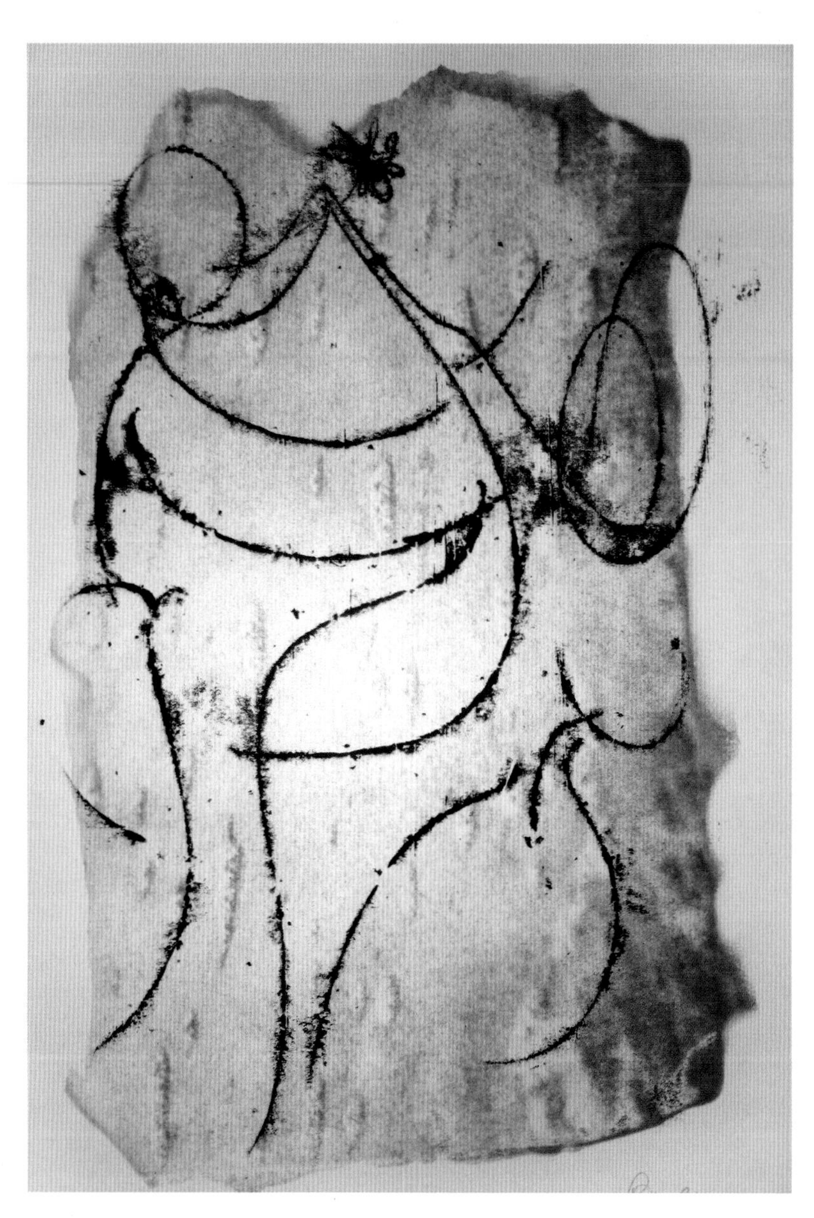

Happy Meeting

(2004) transfer print,
15 1/2 x 10

Bashful

(2004) transfer print,
10 1/2 x 8 1/2

One Step at a Time

(2004) transfer print,
11 1/2 x 8 1/2

Awkward Visit

(2004) transfer print,
14 x 10

Reaching High

(2004) transfer print,
14 1/2 x 10 1/2

Pipe with Friend

(2004) transfer print,
12 3/8 x 9 1/4

When I Grow Up/A Bookperson's Dream

26 miniature etchings (2 x 2), with *pochoir*. An alphabet book dealing with related aspects of creating and collecting books. Etchings and accompanying text by Feldman. Type printed letter press. Signed and numbered. Bound and boxed in slipcase by James Di Marcantonio (Hope Bindery). Edition 26 copies. Copies are in the collections of University of Texas at El Paso, New York Public Library, and Princeton University Rare Book Library.

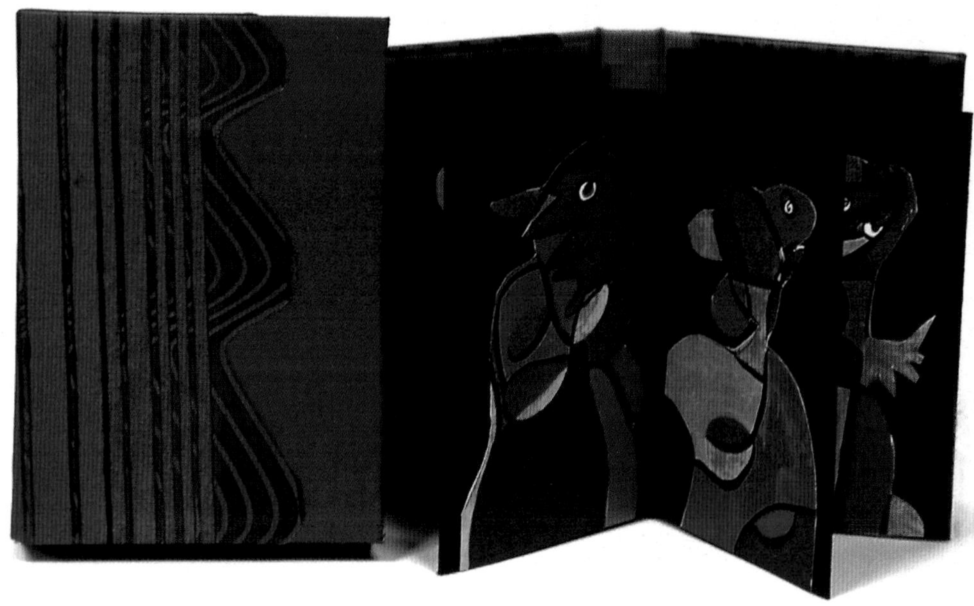

Colorful Friends

Foam core, cut, designed with acrylic. Original set in flip-flap holder-base. Images reduced photographically to form miniature accordion book. Bound and boxed in slipcase by James Di Marcantonio (Hope Bindery). One copy of original and one copy of accordion book.

Dancing in Nature

A multi-layered accordion-plus book with images, offsets, and moving parts. Signed and numbered. Bound and boxed in slipcase by James Di Marcantonio (Hope Bindery). Edition 5 copies.

THE UNUSUAL UBIQUITY OR THE INQUISITIVE GANDER

A gander dwelt upon a farm
And no one could resist him,
For had he died, such was his charm,
His neighbors would have missed him:
His scorn for any loud display,
His cheerful hissing day by day,
Would win your heart in such a way
You almost could have kissed him.

The bird was always, nosing 'round.
Most patiently he waited
Until an open door he found,
And then investigated.

He loved to poke, he loved to peek,
In every knothole, so to speak,
He quickly thrust his prying beak,
For what was hid he hated.

The farm exhausted, "Now," said he:
"My policy's expansion.
When one's convinced how things should be."
The proper course he can't shun.
His mind made up, he followed it,
Relying on his native wit,
And soon had wandered, bit by bit,
Through all his master's mansion.

"At least," he said: "It's not my fault
If everything's not seen to:
I've gone from garret down to vault,
And glanced into the lean-to.
In every room I've chanced to stop;
A supervising glance to drop,
I've looked below, I've looked on top,
Behind, and in between, too!"

One thing alone he found to blame,
As thus his time he squandered,
For, seeing not the farmer's dame,
Into her room he wandered,
And mounting nimbly on the bed:
"Why, bless my careful soul!" he said:
"These pillows are as hard as lead.
Now, how comes that?" he pondered.

Mother Goose for Grown-Ups by Guy Wetmore Carryl

Silhouettes by Feldman, illustrating six of Carryl's fables and designed by Joan O'Connor. Edition ten copies of which eight are on colored stock and colored cover; two are black on white paper. Signed and numbered. Bound and boxed in slipcase by James Di Marcantonio (Hope Bindery). "Commended" by judges of the Fable Book Competition 2004 and included in Supplement of the Journal of the Fine Press Book Association.